ABOUT THIS TIME TRAVEL WORLD HISTORY JOURNAL

Throughout history the world has seen plenty of heroes and villains. Students love to learn about the "good guy" and the "bad guy." In this journal, kids get to be the judge and decide who is the hero and who is the villain.

Students will research over 30 different historical figures from throughout the world and the ages. For each person the student will learn about their accomplishments, family, life, beliefs, and more. After their research is over they'll decide if that person is a hero or a villain.

Dive into thinking about these influencers in a way no other material out there does. It is a wonderful way to study history that is fun and engaging. Use daily for a unit lasting about 6 weeks, or weekly to last all year. You can even use this over a period of several years as you study different historical periods.

Thinking Tree Learning Levels: C1 & C2, ideal for ages 10+. This journal is an excellent companion to our Make Your Own Timeline of World History.

This book uses the Dyslexie font for easier reading for Dyslexic students.

History is violent, so be aware that studying some of these characters can be quite disturbing.

The Thinking Tree

Time Travel World History

HEROES & VILLAINS

You be the JUDGE

Anna Miriam Brown

Sarah Janisse Brown

Joshua William Brown

Copyright 2019

The Thinking Tree, LLC

FunSchooling.com

THE HEROES & THE VILLAINS:

- George Washington
- Adolf Hitler
- Albert Einstein
- Walt Disney
- Nikola Jurisic
- Josef Mengele
- Alexander the Great
- Elizabeth Schuyler
- Osama Bin Laden
- Charles Martel
- Saddam Hussein
- Augustus
- Amy Carmichael
- Leif Erikson
- Michael Jackson
- Mother Teresa
- Julius Caesar
- Jesus Christ
- George Muller
- Martin Luther King Jr.
- Kim Il-Sung
- Thomas Jefferson

- Benjamin Franklin
- Isaac Newton
- Hudson Taylor
- Caesar Nero
- William Shakespeare
- Abraham Lincoln
- The Apostle Paul
- Rosa Parks
- Vincent van Gogh
- Joseph Stalin
- Napoleon Bonaparte
- Queen Victoria
- Christopher Columbus
- Lottie Moon

- Charles Darwin
- Nicholas Winton
- Leonardo da Vinci
- Ruby Bridges
- Genghis Khan
- Dietrich Bonhoeffer
- Mozart
- Henry Ford
- John Adams
- Saint Nicholas
- Pol Pot
- David Livingstone
- Neil Armstrong
- John Jay

"Only one who devotes himself to a cause with his whole strength and soul can be a true master. For this reason mastery demands all of a person."

Albert Einstein

"If you tell a big enough lie and tell it frequently enough, it will be believed."

Adolf Hitler

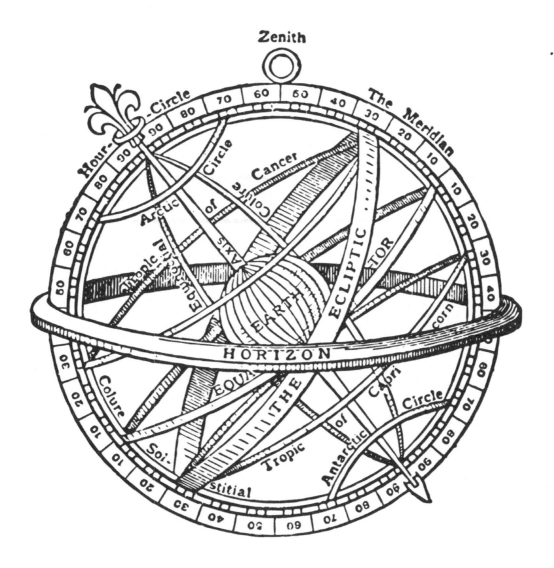

"Before you judge me, try hard to love me, look within your heart. Then ask: have you seen my childhood?"

Michael Jackson

George Washington

Before you start, do you think this person is a hero of history or a villain?
_____

Why?
_____
_____
_____
_____

Draw this person

It's Research Time!

Using Internet search, Wikipedia, documentaries or library books to find answers to the following questions.

What were his goals?
_____
_____
_____
_____

What did he actually accomplish?
_____
_____
_____
_____
_____
_____

Who was his family, and was there anything notable about his upbringing?
_____
_____
_____

Was he married? If so, to whom, and is there anything significant about his spouse? _____
_____

What was his occupation?
_____
_____

In what ways did his life affect our world?
_____
_____
_____
_____

When and where was he born?
_____
_____

When, where, and how did he die?
_____
_____
_____

How would the world be different if he had never been born?
_____
_____
_____
_____
_____
_____

What were his beliefs?
_____
_____
_____
_____
_____
_____
_____
_____
_____
_____

Design a postage stamp to commemorate this person

Random fact about this person:
_____
_____
_____
_____

A quote by this person:
_____
_____
_____
_____

Autobiography

Write a short auto biography from the perspective of the person you are studying.

_____
_____
_____
_____
_____
_____
_____
_____
_____
_____
_____
_____
_____
_____
_____
_____
_____

You be the Judge

Illustrate their life

Now after all your research, would you say this person is a historic hero or villain? Explain in detail.

_____
_____
_____
_____
_____
_____
_____
_____

Adolf Hitler

Before you start, do you think this person is a hero of history or a villain?
_____

Why?
_____
_____
_____
_____

Draw this person

It's Research Time!

Using Internet search, Wikipedia, documentaries or library books to find answers to the following questions.

What were his goals?
_____
_____
_____
_____

What did he actually accomplish?
_____
_____
_____
_____
_____
_____

Who was his family, and was there anything notable about his upbringing?
_____
_____

Was he married? If so, to whom, and is there anything significant about his spouse? _____

What was his occupation?
_____
_____
_____

In what ways did his life affect our world?
_____
_____
_____
_____

When and where was he born?
_____

When, where, and how did he die?
_____
_____

How would the world be different if he had never been born?
_____
_____
_____
_____

What were his beliefs?
_____
_____
_____
_____
_____
_____
_____
_____

Design a postage stamp to commemorate this person

Random fact about this person:
_____
_____
_____

A quote by this person:
_____
_____
_____

Autobiography

Write a short auto biography from the perspective of the person you are studying.

_____
_____
_____
_____
_____
_____
_____
_____
_____
_____
_____
_____
_____
_____
_____
_____

You be the Judge

Illustrate their life

Now after all your research, would you say this person is a historic hero or villain? Explain in detail.

_____
_____
_____
_____
_____
_____
_____

Albert Einstein

Before you start, do you think this person is a hero of history or a villain?

_____

Why?

_____
_____
_____

Draw this person

It's Research Time!

Using Internet search, Wikipedia, documentaries or library books to find answers to the following questions.

What were his goals?
_____
_____
_____
_____

What did he actually accomplish?
_____
_____
_____
_____
_____
_____

Who was his family, and was there anything notable about his upbringing?
_____
_____
_____

Was he married? If so, to whom, and is there anything significant about his spouse? _____
_____

What was his occupation?
_____
_____
_____

In what ways did his life affect our world?
_____
_____
_____
_____
_____

When and where was he born?
_____
_____

When, where, and how did he die?
_____
_____
_____

How would the world be different if he had never been born?
_____
_____
_____
_____
_____

What were his beliefs?
_____
_____
_____
_____
_____
_____
_____
_____
_____

Design a postage stamp to commemorate this person

Random fact about this person:
_____
_____
_____
_____

A quote by this person:
_____
_____
_____
_____

Autobiography

Write a short auto biography from the perspective of the person you are studying.

_____
_____
_____
_____
_____
_____
_____
_____
_____
_____
_____
_____
_____
_____
_____
_____
_____
_____
_____

You be the Judge

Illustrate their life

Now after all your research, would you say this person is a historic hero or villain? Explain in detail.

_____
_____
_____
_____
_____
_____
_____

Walt Disney

Before you start, do you think this person is a hero of history or a villain?
_____

Why?
_____
_____
_____
_____

Draw this person

It's Research Time!

Using Internet search, Wikipedia, documentaries or library books to find answers to the following questions.

What were his goals?
_____
_____
_____
_____

What did he actually accomplish?
_____
_____
_____
_____
_____
_____

Who was his family, and was there anything notable about his upbringing?
_____
_____
_____

Was he married? If so, to whom, and is there anything significant about his spouse? _____
_____

What was his occupation?
_____
_____
_____

In what ways did his life affect our world?
_____
_____
_____
_____

When and where was he born?
_____

When, where, and how did he die?
_____
_____

How would the world be different if he had never been born?
_____
_____
_____
_____

What were his beliefs?
_____
_____
_____
_____
_____
_____
_____
_____

Design a postage stamp to commemorate this person

Random fact about this person:
_____
_____
_____

A quote by this person:
_____
_____
_____
_____

Autobiography

Write a short auto biography from the perspective of the person you are studying.

_____
_____
_____
_____
_____
_____
_____
_____
_____
_____
_____
_____
_____
_____
_____
_____

You be the Judge

Illustrate their life

Now after all your research, would you say this person is a historic hero or villain? Explain in detail.

_____
_____
_____
_____
_____
_____
_____

Nikola Jurišić

Before you start, do you think this person is a hero of history or a villain?
_____

Why?
_____
_____
_____
_____

Draw this person

It's Research Time!

Using Internet search, Wikipedia, documentaries or library books to find answers to the following questions.

What were his goals?
_____
_____
_____
_____

What did he actually accomplish?
_____
_____
_____
_____
_____
_____

Who was his family, and was there anything notable about his upbringing?
_____
_____
_____

Was he married? If so, to whom, and is there anything significant about his spouse? _____
_____

What was his occupation?
_____
_____

In what ways did his life affect our world?
_____
_____
_____
_____

When and where was he born?
_____

When, where, and how did he die?
_____
_____

How would the world be different if he had never been born?
_____
_____
_____
_____

What were his beliefs?
_____
_____
_____
_____
_____
_____
_____
_____

Design a postage stamp to commemorate this person

Random fact about this person:
_____
_____
_____

A quote by this person:
_____
_____
_____
_____

Autobiography

Write a short auto biography from the perspective of the person you are studying.

_____
_____
_____
_____
_____
_____
_____
_____
_____
_____
_____
_____
_____
_____
_____

You be the Judge

Illustrate their life

Now after all your research, would you say this person is a historic hero or villain? Explain in detail.

_____
_____
_____
_____
_____
_____
_____

Josef Mengele

Before you start, do you think this person is a hero of history or a villain?
_____

Why?
_____
_____
_____
_____

Draw this person

It's Research Time!

Using Internet search, Wikipedia, documentaries or library books to find answers to the following questions.

What were his goals?
_____
_____
_____
_____

What did he actually accomplish?
_____
_____
_____
_____
_____
_____

Who was his family, and was there anything notable about his upbringing?
_____
_____
_____

Was he married? If so, to whom, and is there anything significant about his spouse? _____
_____

What was his occupation?
_____
_____

In what ways did his life affect our world?
_____
_____
_____
_____

When and where was he born?
_____

When, where, and how did he die?
_____
_____

How would the world be different if he had never been born?
_____
_____
_____
_____

What were his beliefs?
_____
_____
_____
_____
_____
_____
_____
_____
_____

Design a postage stamp to commemorate this person

Random fact about this person:
_____
_____
_____

A quote by this person:
_____
_____
_____

Autobiography

Write a short auto biography from the perspective of the person you are studying.

_____
_____
_____
_____
_____
_____
_____
_____
_____
_____
_____
_____
_____
_____
_____

You be the Judge

Illustrate their life

Now after all your research, would you say this person is a historic hero or villain? Explain in detail.

_____
_____
_____
_____
_____
_____
_____
_____

Alexander the Great

Before you start, do you think this person is a hero of history or a villain?

_____

Why?

_____
_____
_____
_____

Draw this person

It's Research Time!

Using Internet search, Wikipedia, documentaries or library books to find answers to the following questions.

What were his goals?
_____
_____
_____
_____

What did he actually accomplish?
_____
_____
_____
_____
_____
_____

Who was his family, and was there anything notable about his upbringing?
_____
_____
_____

Was he married? If so, to whom, and is there anything significant about his spouse? _____
_____

What was his occupation?
_____
_____

In what ways did his life affect our world?
_____
_____
_____
_____

When and where was he born?
_____

When, where, and how did he die?
_____
_____

How would the world be different if he had never been born?
_____
_____
_____
_____

What were his beliefs?
_____
_____
_____
_____
_____
_____
_____
_____

Design a postage stamp to commemorate this person

Random fact about this person:
_____
_____
_____

A quote by this person:
_____
_____
_____
_____

Autobiography

Write a short auto biography from the perspective of the person you are studying.

_____
_____
_____
_____
_____
_____
_____
_____
_____
_____
_____
_____
_____
_____
_____
_____

You be the Judge

Illustrate their life

Now after all your research, would you say this person is a historic hero or villain? Explain in detail.

_____
_____
_____
_____
_____
_____
_____
_____

Elizabeth Schuyler

Before you start, do you think this person is a hero of history or a villain?
_____

Why?
_____
_____
_____
_____

Draw this person

It's Research Time!

Using Internet search, Wikipedia, documentaries or library books to find answers to the following questions.

What were her goals?

_____
_____
_____
_____

What did she actually accomplish?

_____
_____
_____
_____
_____

Who was her family, and was there anything notable about her upbringing?

_____
_____
_____

Was she married? If so, to whom, and is there anything significant about her spouse? _____
_____

What was her occupation?

_____
_____
_____

In what ways did her life affect our world?

_____
_____
_____
_____
_____

When and where was she born?
_____

When, where, and how did she die?
_____

How would the world be different if she had never been born?
_____
_____
_____
_____
_____

What were her beliefs?
_____
_____
_____
_____
_____
_____
_____
_____

Design a postage stamp to commemorate this person

Random fact about this person:
_____
_____
_____

A quote by this person:
_____
_____
_____
_____

Autobiography

Write a short auto biography from the perspective of the person you are studying.

_____
_____
_____
_____
_____
_____
_____
_____
_____
_____
_____
_____
_____
_____
_____

You be the Judge

Illustrate their life

Now after all your research, would you say this person is a historic hero or villain? Explain in detail.

_____
_____
_____
_____
_____
_____
_____

Osama Bin Laden

Before you start, do you think this person is a hero of history or a villain?
_____

Why?
_____
_____
_____
_____

Draw this person

It's Research Time!

Using Internet search, Wikipedia, documentaries or library books to find answers to the following questions.

What were his goals?
_____
_____
_____
_____

What did he actually accomplish?
_____
_____
_____
_____
_____
_____

Who was his family, and was there anything notable about his upbringing?
_____
_____
_____

Was he married? If so, to whom, and is there anything significant about his spouse? _____
_____

What was his occupation?
_____
_____
_____

In what ways did his life affect our world?
_____
_____
_____
_____
_____

When and where was he born?
_____

When, where, and how did he die?
_____
_____

How would the world be different if he had never been born?
_____
_____
_____
_____

What were his beliefs?
_____
_____
_____
_____
_____
_____
_____
_____

Design a postage stamp to commemorate this person

Random fact about this person:
_____
_____
_____

A quote by this person:
_____
_____
_____

Autobiography

Write a short auto biography from the perspective of the person you are studying.

_____
_____
_____
_____
_____
_____
_____
_____
_____
_____
_____
_____
_____
_____

You be the Judge

Illustrate their life

Now after all your research, would you say this person is a historic hero or villain? Explain in detail.

_____
_____
_____
_____
_____
_____
_____
_____

Charles Martel

Before you start, do you think this person is a hero of history or a villain?
_____

Why?
_____
_____
_____
_____

Draw this person

It's Research Time!

Using Internet search, Wikipedia, documentaries or library books to find answers to the following questions.

What were his goals?
_____
_____
_____
_____

What did he actually accomplish?
_____
_____
_____
_____
_____
_____
_____

Who was his family, and was there anything notable about his upbringing?
_____
_____
_____

Was he married? If so, to whom, and is there anything significant about his spouse? _____
_____

What was his occupation?
_____
_____
_____

In what ways did his life affect our world?
_____
_____
_____
_____
_____

When and where was he born?
_____

When, where, and how did he die?
_____
_____

How would the world be different if he had never been born?
_____
_____
_____
_____

What were his beliefs?
_____
_____
_____
_____
_____
_____
_____
_____
_____

Design a postage stamp to commemorate this person

Random fact about this person:
_____
_____
_____

A quote by this person:
_____
_____
_____

Autobiography

Write a short auto biography from the perspective of the person you are studying.

_____
_____
_____
_____
_____
_____
_____
_____
_____
_____
_____
_____
_____
_____
_____
_____

You be the Judge

Illustrate their life

Now after all your research, would you say this person is a historic hero or villain? Explain in detail.

_____
_____
_____
_____
_____
_____
_____

Saddam Hussein

Before you start, do you think this person is a hero of history or a villain?

_____

Why?

_____
_____
_____

Draw this person

It's Research Time!

Using Internet search, Wikipedia, documentaries or library books to find answers to the following questions.

What were his goals?
_____
_____
_____
_____

What did he actually accomplish?
_____
_____
_____
_____
_____
_____
_____

Who was his family, and was there anything notable about his upbringing?
_____
_____
_____

Was he married? If so, to whom, and is there anything significant about his spouse? _____
_____

What was his occupation?
_____
_____
_____

In what ways did his life affect our world?
_____
_____
_____
_____
_____
_____

When and where was he born?
_____

When, where, and how did he die?
_____
_____

How would the world be different if he had never been born?
_____
_____
_____
_____

What were his beliefs?
_____
_____
_____
_____
_____
_____
_____
_____

Design a postage stamp to commemorate this person

Random fact about this person:
_____
_____
_____

A quote by this person:
_____
_____
_____
_____

Autobiography

Write a short auto biography from the perspective of the person you are studying.

_____
_____
_____
_____
_____
_____
_____
_____
_____
_____
_____
_____
_____
_____
_____

You be the Judge

Illustrate their life

Now after all your research, would you say this person is a historic hero or villain? Explain in detail.

_____
_____
_____
_____
_____
_____
_____
_____

Augustus

Before you start, do you think this person is a hero of history or a villain?
_____

Why?
_____
_____
_____
_____

Draw this person

It's Research Time!

Using Internet search, Wikipedia, documentaries or library books to find answers to the following questions.

What were his goals?
_____
_____
_____
_____
_____

What did he actually accomplish?
_____
_____
_____
_____
_____
_____
_____

Who was his family, and was there anything notable about his upbringing?
_____
_____
_____

Was he married? If so, to whom, and is there anything significant about his spouse? _____
_____

What was his occupation?
_____
_____
_____

In what ways did his life affect our world?
_____
_____
_____
_____

When and where was he born?
_____

When, where, and how did he die?
_____
_____

How would the world be different if he had never been born?
_____
_____
_____
_____

What were his beliefs?
_____
_____
_____
_____
_____
_____
_____
_____

Design a postage stamp to commemorate this person

Random fact about this person:
_____
_____
_____

A quote by this person:
_____
_____
_____
_____

Autobiography

Write a short auto biography from the perspective of the person you are studying.

_____
_____
_____
_____
_____
_____
_____
_____
_____
_____
_____
_____
_____
_____
_____

You be the Judge

Illustrate their life

Now after all your research, would you say this person is a historic hero or villain? Explain in detail.

_____
_____
_____
_____
_____
_____
_____

Amy Carmichael

Before you start, do you think this person is a hero of history or a villain?
_____

Why?
_____
_____
_____
_____

Draw this person

It's Research Time!

Using Internet search, Wikipedia, documentaries or library books to find answers to the following questions.

What were her goals?
_____
_____
_____
_____
_____

What did she actually accomplish?
_____
_____
_____
_____
_____

Who was her family, and was there anything notable about her upbringing?
_____
_____
_____

Was she married? If so, to whom, and is there anything significant about her spouse? _____
_____

What was her occupation?
_____
_____
_____

In what ways did her life affect our world?
_____
_____
_____
_____
_____

When and where was she born?
_____

When, where, and how did she die?
_____

How would the world be different if she had never been born?
_____
_____
_____
_____

What were her beliefs?
_____
_____
_____
_____
_____
_____
_____
_____

Design a postage stamp to commemorate this person

Random fact about this person:
_____
_____
_____

A quote by this person:
_____
_____
_____

Autobiography

Write a short auto biography from the perspective of the person you are studying.

_____
_____
_____
_____
_____
_____
_____
_____
_____
_____
_____
_____
_____
_____
_____
_____
_____
_____
_____

You be the Judge

Illustrate their life

Now after all your research, would you say this person is a historic hero or villain? Explain in detail.

_____
_____
_____
_____
_____
_____
_____

Leif Erikson

Before you start, do you think this person is a hero of history or a villain?
_____

Why?
_____
_____
_____
_____

Draw this person

It's Research Time!

Using Internet search, Wikipedia, documentaries or library books to find answers to the following questions.

What were his goals?
_____
_____
_____
_____

What did he actually accomplish?
_____
_____
_____
_____
_____
_____

Who was his family, and was there anything notable about his upbringing?
_____
_____
_____

Was he married? If so, to whom, and is there anything significant about his spouse? _____
_____

What was his occupation?
_____
_____
_____

In what ways did his life affect our world?
_____
_____
_____
_____

When and where was he born?
_____

When, where, and how did he die?
_____
_____

How would the world be different if he had never been born?
_____
_____
_____
_____

What were his beliefs?
_____
_____
_____
_____
_____
_____
_____
_____
_____

Design a postage stamp to commemorate this person

Random fact about this person:
_____
_____
_____

A quote by this person:
_____
_____
_____

Autobiography

Write a short auto biography from the perspective of the person you are studying.

_____
_____
_____
_____
_____
_____
_____
_____
_____
_____
_____
_____
_____
_____
_____
_____

You be the Judge

Illustrate their life

Now after all your research, would you say this person is a historic hero or villain? Explain in detail.

_____
_____
_____
_____
_____
_____
_____

Michael Jackson

Before you start, do you think this person is a hero of history or a villain?

Why?

Draw this person

It's Research Time!

Using Internet search, Wikipedia, documentaries or library books to find answers to the following questions.

What were his goals?
_____
_____
_____
_____

What did he actually accomplish?
_____
_____
_____
_____
_____

Who was his family, and was there anything notable about his upbringing?
_____
_____
_____

Was he married? If so, to whom, and is there anything significant about his spouse? _____
_____

What was his occupation?
_____
_____
_____

In what ways did his life affect our world?
_____
_____
_____
_____

When and where was he born?
_____

When, where, and how did he die?
_____
_____

How would the world be different if he had never been born?
_____
_____
_____
_____

What were his beliefs?
_____
_____
_____
_____
_____
_____
_____
_____

Design a postage stamp to commemorate this person

Random fact about this person:
_____
_____
_____

A quote by this person:
_____
_____
_____
_____

Autobiography

Write a short auto biography from the perspective of the person you are studying.

_____
_____
_____
_____
_____
_____
_____
_____
_____
_____
_____
_____
_____
_____
_____

You be the Judge

Illustrate their life

Now after all your research, would you say this person is a historic hero or villain? Explain in detail.

_____
_____
_____
_____
_____
_____
_____

Mother Teresa

Before you start, do you think this person is a hero of history or a villain?

_____

Why?

_____
_____
_____
_____

Draw this person

It's Research Time!

Using Internet search, Wikipedia, documentaries or library books to find answers to the following questions.

What were her goals?
_____
_____
_____
_____
_____

What did she actually accomplish?
_____
_____
_____
_____
_____

Who was her family, and was there anything notable about her upbringing?
_____
_____
_____

Was she married? If so, to whom, and is there anything significant about her spouse? _____
_____
_____

What was her occupation?
_____
_____
_____

In what ways did her life affect our world?
_____
_____
_____
_____
_____

When and where was she born?
_____

When, where, and how did she die?
_____

How would the world be different if she had never been born?
_____
_____
_____
_____
_____

What were her beliefs?
_____
_____
_____
_____
_____
_____
_____

Design a postage stamp to commemorate this person

Random fact about this person:
_____
_____
_____

A quote by this person:
_____
_____
_____

Autobiography

Write a short auto biography from the perspective of the person you are studying.

_____
_____
_____
_____
_____
_____
_____
_____
_____
_____
_____
_____
_____
_____

You be the Judge

Illustrate their life

Now after all your research, would you say this person is a historic hero or villain? Explain in detail.

_____
_____
_____
_____
_____
_____
_____

Julius Caesar

Before you start, do you think this person is a hero of history or a villain?
_____

Why?
_____
_____
_____
_____

Draw this person

It's Research Time!

Using Internet search, Wikipedia, documentaries or library books to find answers to the following questions.

What were his goals?
_____
_____
_____
_____

What did he actually accomplish?
_____
_____
_____
_____
_____
_____

Who was his family, and was there anything notable about his upbringing?
_____
_____
_____

Was he married? If so, to whom, and is there anything significant about his spouse? _____
_____

What was his occupation?
_____
_____
_____

In what ways did his life affect our world?
_____
_____
_____
_____

When and where was he born?
_____

When, where, and how did he die?
_____
_____

How would the world be different if he had never been born?
_____
_____
_____
_____

What were his beliefs?
_____
_____
_____
_____
_____
_____
_____
_____

Design a postage stamp to commemorate this person

Random fact about this person:
_____
_____
_____

A quote by this person:
_____
_____
_____

Autobiography

Write a short auto biography from the perspective of the person you are studying.

_____
_____
_____
_____
_____
_____
_____
_____
_____
_____
_____
_____
_____
_____
_____
_____

You be the Judge

Illustrate their life

Now after all your research, would you say this person is a historic hero or villain? Explain in detail.

_____
_____
_____
_____
_____
_____

Jesus Christ

Before you start, do you think this person is a hero of history or a villain?
_____

Why?
_____
_____
_____
_____

Draw this person

It's Research Time!

Using Internet search, Wikipedia, documentaries or library books to find answers to the following questions.

What were his goals?
_____
_____
_____
_____

What did he actually accomplish?
_____
_____
_____
_____
_____
_____

Who was his family, and was there anything notable about his upbringing?
_____
_____
_____

Was he married? If so, to whom, and is there anything significant about his spouse? _____
_____

What was his occupation?
_____
_____
_____

In what ways did his life affect our world?
_____
_____
_____
_____
_____

When and where was he born?
_____
_____

When, where, and how did he die?
_____
_____

How would the world be different if he had never been born?
_____
_____
_____
_____
_____

What were his beliefs?
_____
_____
_____
_____
_____
_____
_____
_____
_____

Design a postage stamp to commemorate this person

Random fact about this person:
_____
_____
_____
_____

A quote by this person:
_____
_____
_____
_____

Autobiography

Write a short auto biography from the perspective of the person you are studying.

_____
_____
_____
_____
_____
_____
_____
_____
_____
_____
_____
_____
_____
_____
_____

You be the Judge

Illustrate their life

Now after all your research, would you say this person is a historic hero or villain? Explain in detail.

_____
_____
_____
_____
_____
_____
_____

George Müller

Before you start, do you think this person is a hero of history or a villain?
_____

Why?
_____
_____
_____
_____

Draw this person

It's Research Time!

Using Internet search, Wikipedia, documentaries or library books to find answers to the following questions.

What were his goals?
_____
_____
_____
_____

What did he actually accomplish?
_____
_____
_____
_____
_____
_____

Who was his family, and was there anything notable about his upbringing?
_____
_____
_____

Was he married? If so, to whom, and is there anything significant about his spouse? _____
_____

What was his occupation?
_____
_____
_____

In what ways did his life affect our world?
_____
_____
_____
_____
_____

When and where was he born?
_____

When, where, and how did he die?
_____
_____

How would the world be different if he had never been born?
_____
_____
_____
_____

What were his beliefs?
_____
_____
_____
_____
_____
_____
_____
_____
_____

Design a postage stamp to commemorate this person

Random fact about this person:
_____
_____
_____

A quote by this person:
_____
_____
_____
_____

Autobiography

Write a short auto biography from the perspective of the person you are studying.

_____
_____
_____
_____
_____
_____
_____
_____
_____
_____
_____
_____
_____
_____

You be the Judge

Illustrate their life

Now after all your research, would you say this person is a historic hero or villain? Explain in detail.

_____
_____
_____
_____
_____
_____
_____

Martin Luther King Jr.

Before you start, do you think this person is a hero of history or a villain?

Why?

Draw this person

It's Research Time!

Using Internet search, Wikipedia, documentaries or library books to find answers to the following questions.

What were his goals?
_____
_____
_____
_____
_____

What did he actually accomplish?
_____
_____
_____
_____
_____
_____
_____

Who was his family, and was there anything notable about his upbringing?
_____
_____
_____

Was he married? If so, to whom, and is there anything significant about his spouse? _____
_____

What was his occupation?
_____
_____
_____

In what ways did his life affect our world?
_____
_____
_____
_____
_____

When and where was he born?
_____

When, where, and how did he die?
_____
_____

How would the world be different if he had never been born?
_____
_____
_____
_____

What were his beliefs?
_____
_____
_____
_____
_____
_____
_____
_____

Design a postage stamp to commemorate this person

Random fact about this person:
_____
_____
_____

A quote by this person:
_____
_____
_____
_____

Autobiography

Write a short auto biography from the perspective of the person you are studying.

_____
_____
_____
_____
_____
_____
_____
_____
_____
_____
_____
_____
_____

You be the Judge

Illustrate their life

Now after all your research, would you say this person is a historic hero or villain? Explain in detail.

_____
_____
_____
_____
_____
_____
_____

Kim Il-Sung

Before you start, do you think this person is a hero of history or a villain?
_____

Why?
_____
_____
_____
_____

Draw this person

It's Research Time!

Using Internet search, Wikipedia, documentaries or library books to find answers to the following questions.

What were his goals?
_____
_____
_____
_____
_____

What did he actually accomplish?
_____
_____
_____
_____
_____
_____
_____
_____

Who was his family, and was there anything notable about his upbringing?
_____
_____
_____

Was he married? If so, to whom, and is there anything significant about his spouse? _____
_____

What was his occupation?
_____
_____
_____

In what ways did his life affect our world?
_____
_____
_____
_____
_____

When and where was he born?

When, where, and how did he die?

How would the world be different if he had never been born?

What were his beliefs?

Random fact about this person:

A quote by this person:

Design a postage stamp to commemorate this person

Autobiography

Write a short auto biography from the perspective of the person you are studying.

_____
_____
_____
_____
_____
_____
_____
_____
_____
_____
_____
_____
_____
_____
_____
_____

You be the Judge

Illustrate their life

Now after all your research, would you say this person is a historic hero or villain? Explain in detail.

_____
_____
_____
_____
_____
_____
_____

Thomas Jefferson

Before you start, do you think this person is a hero of history or a villain?

_____

Why?

_____
_____
_____
_____

Draw this person

It's Research Time!

Using Internet search, Wikipedia, documentaries or library books to find answers to the following questions.

What were his goals?
_____
_____
_____
_____
_____

What did he actually accomplish?
_____
_____
_____
_____
_____

Who was his family, and was there anything notable about his upbringing?
_____
_____
_____

Was he married? If so, to whom, and is there anything significant about his spouse? _____
_____

What was his occupation?
_____
_____

In what ways did his life affect our world?
_____
_____
_____
_____

When and where was he born?
_____

When, where, and how did he die?
_____
_____

How would the world be different if he had never been born?
_____
_____
_____
_____

What were his beliefs?
_____
_____
_____
_____
_____
_____
_____

Design a postage stamp to commemorate this person

Random fact about this person:
_____
_____
_____

A quote by this person:
_____
_____
_____
_____

Autobiography

Write a short auto biography from the perspective of the person you are studying.

_____
_____
_____
_____
_____
_____
_____
_____
_____
_____
_____
_____
_____
_____
_____
_____
_____

You be the Judge

Illustrate their life

Now after all your research, would you say this person is a historic hero or villain? Explain in detail.

_____
_____
_____
_____
_____
_____
_____

Benjamin Franklin

Before you start, do you think this person is a hero of history or a villain?
_____

Why?
_____
_____
_____
_____

Draw this person

It's Research Time!

Using Internet search, Wikipedia, documentaries or library books to find answers to the following questions.

What were his goals?
_____
_____
_____
_____
_____

What did he actually accomplish?
_____
_____
_____
_____
_____
_____

Who was his family, and was there anything notable about his upbringing?
_____
_____
_____

Was he married? If so, to whom, and is there anything significant about his spouse? _____
_____

What was his occupation?
_____
_____
_____

In what ways did his life affect our world?
_____
_____
_____
_____

When and where was he born?
_____

When, where, and how did he die?
_____
_____

How would the world be different if he had never been born?
_____
_____
_____
_____

What were his beliefs?
_____
_____
_____
_____
_____
_____
_____

Design a postage stamp to commemorate this person

Random fact about this person:
_____
_____
_____

A quote by this person:
_____
_____
_____

Autobiography

Write a short auto biography from the perspective of the person you are studying.

_____
_____
_____
_____
_____
_____
_____
_____
_____
_____
_____
_____
_____
_____
_____
_____
_____

You be the Judge

Illustrate their life

Now after all your research, would you say this person is a historic hero or villain? Explain in detail.

_____
_____
_____
_____
_____
_____

Isaac Newton

Before you start, do you think this person is a hero of history or a villain?
_____

Why?
_____
_____
_____

Draw this person

It's Research Time!

Using Internet search, Wikipedia, documentaries or library books to find answers to the following questions.

What were his goals?
_____
_____
_____
_____

What did he actually accomplish?
_____
_____
_____
_____
_____
_____

Who was his family, and was there anything notable about his upbringing?
_____
_____
_____

Was he married? If so, to whom, and is there anything significant about his spouse? _____
_____

What was his occupation?
_____
_____

In what ways did his life affect our world?
_____
_____
_____
_____

When and where was he born?
_____

When, where, and how did he die?
_____
_____

How would the world be different if he had never been born?
_____
_____
_____
_____
_____

What were his beliefs?
_____
_____
_____
_____
_____
_____
_____
_____

Design a postage stamp to commemorate this person

Random fact about this person:
_____
_____
_____

A quote by this person:
_____
_____
_____
_____

Autobiography

Write a short auto biography from the perspective of the person you are studying.

_____
_____
_____
_____
_____
_____
_____
_____
_____
_____
_____
_____
_____
_____
_____
_____

You be the Judge

Illustrate their life

Now after all your research, would you say this person is a historic hero or villain? Explain in detail.

_____
_____
_____
_____
_____
_____
_____

Hudson Taylor

Before you start, do you think this person is a hero of history or a villain?
_____

Why?
_____
_____
_____
_____

Draw this person

It's Research Time!

Using Internet search, Wikipedia, documentaries or library books to find answers to the following questions.

What were his goals?
_____
_____
_____
_____
_____

What did he actually accomplish?
_____
_____
_____
_____
_____
_____

Who was his family, and was there anything notable about his upbringing?
_____
_____
_____

Was he married? If so, to whom, and is there anything significant about his spouse? _____
_____

What was his occupation?
_____
_____
_____

In what ways did his life affect our world?
_____
_____
_____
_____

When and where was he born?
_____

When, where, and how did he die?
_____
_____

How would the world be different if he had never been born?
_____
_____
_____
_____

What were his beliefs?
_____
_____
_____
_____
_____
_____
_____
_____

Design a postage stamp to commemorate this person

Random fact about this person:
_____
_____
_____

A quote by this person:
_____
_____
_____
_____

Autobiography

Write a short auto biography from the perspective of the person you are studying.

_____
_____
_____
_____
_____
_____
_____
_____
_____
_____
_____
_____
_____
_____
_____

You be the Judge

Illustrate their life

Now after all your research, would you say this person is a historic hero or villain? Explain in detail.

_____
_____
_____
_____
_____
_____
_____

Caesar Nero

Before you start, do you think this person is a hero of history or a villain?
_____

Why?
_____
_____
_____
_____

Draw this person

It's Research Time!

Using Internet search, Wikipedia, documentaries or library books to find answers to the following questions.

What were his goals?
_____
_____
_____
_____

What did he actually accomplish?
_____
_____
_____
_____
_____

Who was his family, and was there anything notable about his upbringing?
_____
_____
_____

Was he married? If so, to whom, and is there anything significant about his spouse? _____
_____

What was his occupation?
_____
_____

In what ways did his life affect our world?
_____
_____
_____
_____

When and where was he born?
_____

When, where, and how did he die?
_____
_____

How would the world be different if he had never been born?
_____
_____
_____
_____

What were his beliefs?
_____
_____
_____
_____
_____
_____
_____
_____

Design a postage stamp to commemorate this person

Random fact about this person:
_____
_____
_____

A quote by this person:
_____
_____
_____
_____

Autobiography

Write a short auto biography from the perspective of the person you are studying.

_____
_____
_____
_____
_____
_____
_____
_____
_____
_____
_____
_____
_____
_____
_____
_____
_____

You be the Judge

Illustrate their life

Now after all your research, would you say this person is a historic hero or villain? Explain in detail.

_____
_____
_____
_____
_____
_____

William Shakespeare

Before you start, do you think this person is a hero of history or a villain?
_____

Why?
_____
_____
_____
_____

Draw this person

It's Research Time!

Using Internet search, Wikipedia, documentaries or library books to find answers to the following questions.

What were his goals?
_____
_____
_____
_____
_____

What did he actually accomplish?
_____
_____
_____
_____
_____
_____

Who was his family, and was there anything notable about his upbringing?
_____
_____
_____

Was he married? If so, to whom, and is there anything significant about his spouse? _____
_____

What was his occupation?
_____
_____
_____

In what ways did his life affect our world?
_____
_____
_____
_____

When and where was he born?
_____

When, where, and how did he die?
_____
_____

How would the world be different if he had never been born?
_____
_____
_____
_____

What were his beliefs?
_____
_____
_____
_____
_____
_____
_____
_____

Design a postage stamp to commemorate this person

Random fact about this person:
_____
_____
_____

A quote by this person:
_____
_____
_____

Autobiography

Write a short auto biography from the perspective of the person you are studying.

_____
_____
_____
_____
_____
_____
_____
_____
_____
_____
_____
_____
_____
_____
_____

You be the Judge

Illustrate their life

Now after all your research, would you say this person is a historic hero or villain? Explain in detail.

_____
_____
_____
_____
_____
_____
_____

Abraham Lincoln

Before you start, do you think this person is a hero of history or a villain?
_____

Why?
_____
_____
_____
_____

Draw this person

It's Research Time!

Using Internet search, Wikipedia, documentaries or library books to find answers to the following questions.

What were his goals?
_____
_____
_____
_____

What did he actually accomplish?
_____
_____
_____
_____
_____
_____

Who was his family, and was there anything notable about his upbringing?
_____
_____
_____

Was he married? If so, to whom, and is there anything significant about his spouse? _____
_____

What was his occupation?
_____
_____
_____

In what ways did his life affect our world?
_____
_____
_____
_____

When and where was he born?
_____

When, where, and how did he die?
_____
_____

How would the world be different if he had never been born?
_____
_____
_____
_____

What were his beliefs?
_____
_____
_____
_____
_____
_____
_____
_____
_____

Design a postage stamp to commemorate this person

Random fact about this person:
_____
_____
_____

A quote by this person:
_____
_____
_____
_____

Autobiography

Write a short auto biography from the perspective of the person you are studying.

_____
_____
_____
_____
_____
_____
_____
_____
_____
_____
_____
_____
_____
_____
_____
_____
_____

You be the Judge

Illustrate their life

Now after all your research, would you say this person is a historic hero or villain? Explain in detail.

_____
_____
_____
_____
_____
_____
_____

The Apostle Paul

Before you start, do you think this person is a hero of history or a villain?
_____

Why?
_____
_____
_____
_____

Draw this person

It's Research Time!

Using Internet search, Wikipedia, documentaries or library books to find answers to the following questions.

What were his goals?
_____
_____
_____
_____

What did he actually accomplish?
_____
_____
_____
_____
_____

Who was his family, and was there anything notable about his upbringing?
_____
_____
_____

Was he married? If so, to whom, and is there anything significant about his spouse? _____
_____

What was his occupation?
_____
_____
_____

In what ways did his life affect our world?
_____
_____
_____
_____

When and where was he born?
_____

When, where, and how did he die?
_____
_____

How would the world be different if he had never been born?
_____
_____
_____
_____

What were his beliefs?
_____
_____
_____
_____
_____
_____
_____
_____

Design a postage stamp to commemorate this person

Random fact about this person:
_____
_____
_____

A quote by this person:
_____
_____
_____
_____

Autobiography

Write a short auto biography from the perspective of the person you are studying.

_____
_____
_____
_____
_____
_____
_____
_____
_____
_____
_____
_____
_____
_____

You be the Judge

Illustrate their life

Now after all your research, would you say this person is a historic hero or villain? Explain in detail.

_____
_____
_____
_____
_____
_____

Rosa Parks

Before you start, do you think this person is a hero of history or a villain?

Why?

Draw this person

It's Research Time!

Using Internet search, Wikipedia, documentaries or library books to find answers to the following questions.

What were her goals?
_____
_____
_____
_____
_____

What did she actually accomplish?
_____
_____
_____
_____
_____
_____

Who was her family, and was there anything notable about her upbringing?
_____
_____
_____

Was she married? If so, to whom, and is there anything significant about her spouse? _____
_____

What was her occupation?
_____
_____
_____

In what ways did her life affect our world?
_____
_____
_____
_____
_____

When and where was she born?
_____

When, where, and how did she die?
_____

How would the world be different if she had never been born?
_____
_____
_____
_____
_____

What were her beliefs?
_____
_____
_____
_____
_____
_____
_____
_____
_____

Design a postage stamp to commemorate this person

Random fact about this person:
_____
_____
_____

A quote by this person:
_____
_____
_____

Autobiography

Write a short auto biography from the perspective of the person you are studying.

_____
_____
_____
_____
_____
_____
_____
_____
_____
_____
_____
_____
_____
_____
_____
_____
_____
_____

You be the Judge

Illustrate their life

Now after all your research, would you say this person is a historic hero or villain? Explain in detail.

_____
_____
_____
_____
_____
_____
_____
_____

Vincent van Gogh

Before you start, do you think this person is a hero of history or a villain?
_____

Why?
_____
_____
_____

Draw this person

It's Research Time!

Using Internet search, Wikipedia, documentaries or library books to find answers to the following questions.

What were his goals?
_____
_____
_____
_____
_____

What did he actually accomplish?
_____
_____
_____
_____
_____
_____
_____

Who was his family, and was there anything notable about his upbringing?
_____
_____
_____

Was he married? If so, to whom, and is there anything significant about his spouse? _____
_____

What was his occupation?
_____
_____
_____

In what ways did his life affect our world?
_____
_____
_____
_____
_____

When and where was he born?
_____

When, where, and how did he die?
_____
_____

How would the world be different if he had never been born?
_____
_____
_____
_____

What were his beliefs?
_____
_____
_____
_____
_____
_____
_____
_____
_____

Design a postage stamp to commemorate this person

Random fact about this person:
_____
_____
_____

A quote by this person:
_____
_____
_____

Autobiography

Write a short auto biography from the perspective of the person you are studying.

_____
_____
_____
_____
_____
_____
_____
_____
_____
_____
_____
_____
_____
_____
_____
_____

You be the Judge

Illustrate their life

Now after all your research, would you say this person is a historic hero or villain? Explain in detail.

_____
_____
_____
_____
_____
_____
_____

Joseph Stalin

Before you start, do you think this person is a hero of history or a villain?

Why?

Draw this person

It's Research Time!

Using Internet search, Wikipedia, documentaries or library books to find answers to the following questions.

What were his goals?
_____
_____
_____
_____
_____

What did he actually accomplish?
_____
_____
_____
_____
_____
_____
_____

Who was his family, and was there anything notable about his upbringing?
_____
_____
_____

Was he married? If so, to whom, and is there anything significant about his spouse? _____
_____

What was his occupation?
_____
_____
_____

In what ways did his life affect our world?
_____
_____
_____
_____
_____

When and where was he born?
_____
_____

When, where, and how did he die?
_____
_____

How would the world be different if he had never been born?
_____
_____
_____
_____

What were his beliefs?
_____
_____
_____
_____
_____
_____
_____
_____

Design a postage stamp to commemorate this person

Random fact about this person:
_____
_____
_____

A quote by this person:
_____
_____
_____

Autobiography

Write a short auto biography from the perspective of the person you are studying.

_____
_____
_____
_____
_____
_____
_____
_____
_____
_____
_____
_____
_____
_____
_____
_____

You be the Judge

Illustrate their life

Now after all your research, would you say this person is a historic hero or villain? Explain in detail.

_____
_____
_____
_____
_____
_____
_____

Napoleon Bonaparte

Before you start, do you think this person is a hero of history or a villain?
_____

Why?
_____
_____
_____
_____

Draw this person

It's Research Time!

Using Internet search, Wikipedia, documentaries or library books to find answers to the following questions.

What were his goals?
_____
_____
_____
_____
_____

What did he actually accomplish?
_____
_____
_____
_____
_____
_____

Who was his family, and was there anything notable about his upbringing?
_____
_____
_____

Was he married? If so, to whom, and is there anything significant about his spouse? _____
_____

What was his occupation?
_____
_____
_____

In what ways did his life affect our world?
_____
_____
_____
_____
_____

When and where was he born?
_____

When, where, and how did he die?
_____
_____

How would the world be different if he had never been born?
_____
_____
_____
_____

What were his beliefs?
_____
_____
_____
_____
_____
_____
_____
_____

Design a postage stamp to commemorate this person

Random fact about this person:
_____
_____
_____

A quote by this person:
_____
_____
_____

Autobiography

Write a short auto biography from the perspective of the person you are studying.

_____
_____
_____
_____
_____
_____
_____
_____
_____
_____
_____
_____
_____
_____
_____
_____
_____

You be the Judge

Illustrate their life

Now after all your research, would you say this person is a historic hero or villain? Explain in detail.

_____
_____
_____
_____
_____
_____
_____

Queen Victoria

Before you start, do you think this person is a hero of history or a villain?
_____

Why?
_____
_____
_____
_____

Draw this person

It's Research Time!

Using Internet search, Wikipedia, documentaries or library books to find answers to the following questions.

What were her goals?
_____
_____
_____
_____
_____

What did she actually accomplish?
_____
_____
_____
_____
_____
_____

Who was her family, and was there anything notable about her upbringing?
_____
_____
_____

Was she married? If so, to whom, and is there anything significant about her spouse? _____
_____
_____

What was her occupation?
_____
_____
_____

In what ways did her life affect our world?
_____
_____
_____
_____
_____
_____

When and where was she born?
_____

When, where, and how did she die?
_____

How would the world be different if she had never been born?
_____
_____
_____
_____
_____

What were her beliefs?
_____
_____
_____
_____
_____
_____
_____
_____
_____
_____

Design a postage stamp to commemorate this person

Random fact about this person:
_____
_____
_____
_____

A quote by this person:
_____
_____
_____
_____

Autobiography

Write a short auto biography from the perspective of the person you are studying.

_____
_____
_____
_____
_____
_____
_____
_____
_____
_____
_____
_____
_____
_____
_____

You be the Judge

Illustrate their life

Now after all your research, would you say this person is a historic hero or villain? Explain in detail.

_____
_____
_____
_____
_____
_____
_____

Christopher Columbus

Before you start, do you think this person is a hero of history or a villain?

_____

Why?

_____
_____
_____
_____

Draw this person

It's Research Time!

Using Internet search, Wikipedia, documentaries or library books to find answers to the following questions.

What were his goals?
_____
_____
_____
_____

What did he actually accomplish?
_____
_____
_____
_____
_____
_____

Who was his family, and was there anything notable about his upbringing?
_____
_____
_____

Was he married? If so, to whom, and is there anything significant about his spouse? _____
_____

What was his occupation?
_____
_____
_____

In what ways did his life affect our world?
_____
_____
_____
_____
_____

When and where was he born?
_____

When, where, and how did he die?
_____
_____

How would the world be different if he had never been born?
_____
_____
_____
_____
_____

What were his beliefs?
_____
_____
_____
_____
_____
_____
_____
_____
_____

Design a postage stamp to commemorate this person

Random fact about this person:
_____
_____
_____

A quote by this person:
_____
_____
_____
_____

Autobiography

Write a short auto biography from the perspective of the person you are studying.

_____
_____
_____
_____
_____
_____
_____
_____
_____
_____
_____
_____
_____
_____

You be the Judge

illustrate their life

Now after all your research, would you say this person is a historic hero or villain? Explain in detail.

_____
_____
_____
_____
_____
_____

Lottie Moon

Before you start, do you think this person is a hero of history or a villain?
_____

Why?
_____
_____
_____
_____

Draw this person

It's Research Time!

Using Internet search, Wikipedia, documentaries or library books to find answers to the following questions.

What were her goals?
_____
_____
_____
_____
_____

What did she actually accomplish?
_____
_____
_____
_____
_____
_____

Who was her family, and was there anything notable about her upbringing?
_____
_____
_____
_____

Was she married? If so, to whom, and is there anything significant about her spouse? _____
_____

What was her occupation?
_____
_____
_____

In what ways did her life affect our world?
_____
_____
_____
_____
_____
_____

When and where was she born?
_____

When, where, and how did she die?
_____

How would the world be different if she had never been born?
_____
_____
_____
_____
_____

What were her beliefs?
_____
_____
_____
_____
_____
_____
_____
_____

Design a postage stamp to commemorate this person

Random fact about this person:
_____
_____
_____
_____

A quote by this person:
_____
_____
_____
_____

Autobiography

Write a short auto biography from the perspective of the person you are studying.

_____
_____
_____
_____
_____
_____
_____
_____
_____
_____
_____
_____
_____
_____
_____

You be the Judge

Illustrate their life

Now after all your research, would you say this person is a historic hero or villain? Explain in detail.

_____
_____
_____
_____
_____
_____
_____

Charles Darwin

Before you start, do you think this person is a hero of history or a villain?

_____

Why?

_____
_____
_____
_____

Draw this person

It's Research Time!

Using Internet search, Wikipedia, documentaries or library books to find answers to the following questions.

What were his goals?
_____
_____
_____
_____
_____

What did he actually accomplish?
_____
_____
_____
_____
_____
_____
_____

Who was his family, and was there anything notable about his upbringing?
_____
_____
_____

Was he married? If so, to whom, and is there anything significant about his spouse? _____
_____

What was his occupation?
_____
_____
_____

In what ways did his life affect our world?
_____
_____
_____
_____
_____

When and where was he born?
_____

When, where, and how did he die?
_____
_____

How would the world be different if he had never been born?
_____
_____
_____
_____

What were his beliefs?
_____
_____
_____
_____
_____
_____
_____

Design a postage stamp to commemorate this person

Random fact about this person:
_____
_____
_____

A quote by this person:
_____
_____
_____

Autobiography

Write a short auto biography from the perspective of the person you are studying.

_____
_____
_____
_____
_____
_____
_____
_____
_____
_____
_____
_____
_____
_____
_____
_____

You be the Judge

Illustrate their life

Now after all your research, would you say this person is a historic hero or villain? Explain in detail.

_____
_____
_____
_____
_____
_____
_____

Nicholas Winton

Before you start, do you think this person is a hero of history or a villain?
_____

Why?
_____
_____
_____
_____

Draw this person

It's Research Time!

Using Internet search, Wikipedia, documentaries or library books to find answers to the following questions.

What were his goals?
_____
_____
_____
_____
_____

What did he actually accomplish?
_____
_____
_____
_____
_____
_____

Who was his family, and was there anything notable about his upbringing?
_____
_____
_____

Was he married? If so, to whom, and is there anything significant about his spouse? _____
_____

What was his occupation?
_____
_____
_____

In what ways did his life affect our world?
_____
_____
_____
_____
_____

When and where was he born?
_____

When, where, and how did he die?
_____
_____

How would the world be different if he had never been born?
_____
_____
_____
_____

What were his beliefs?
_____
_____
_____
_____
_____
_____
_____
_____

Design a postage stamp to commemorate this person

Random fact about this person:
_____
_____
_____

A quote by this person:
_____
_____
_____
_____

Autobiography

Write a short auto biography from the perspective of the person you are studying.

_____
_____
_____
_____
_____
_____
_____
_____
_____
_____
_____
_____
_____
_____

You be the Judge

Illustrate their life

Now after all your research, would you say this person is a historic hero or villain? Explain in detail.

_____
_____
_____
_____
_____
_____
_____

Leonardo da Vinci

Before you start, do you think this person is a hero of history or a villain?
_____

Why?
_____
_____
_____
_____

Draw this person

It's Research Time!

Using Internet search, Wikipedia, documentaries or library books to find answers to the following questions.

What were his goals?
_____
_____
_____
_____

What did he actually accomplish?
_____
_____
_____
_____
_____
_____

Who was his family, and was there anything notable about his upbringing?
_____
_____
_____

Was he married? If so, to whom, and is there anything significant about his spouse? _____

What was his occupation?
_____
_____
_____

In what ways did his life affect our world?
_____
_____
_____
_____
_____

When and where was he born?
_____

When, where, and how did he die?
_____
_____

How would the world be different if he had never been born?
_____
_____
_____
_____

What were his beliefs?
_____
_____
_____
_____
_____
_____
_____

Design a postage stamp to commemorate this person

Random fact about this person:
_____
_____
_____

A quote by this person:
_____
_____
_____

Autobiography

Write a short auto biography from the perspective of the person you are studying.

_____
_____
_____
_____
_____
_____
_____
_____
_____
_____
_____
_____
_____
_____
_____

You be the Judge

Illustrate their life

Now after all your research, would you say this person is a historic hero or villain? Explain in detail.

_____
_____
_____
_____
_____
_____

Ruby Bridges

Before you start, do you think this person is a hero of history or a villain?
_____

Why?
_____
_____
_____
_____

Draw this person

It's Research Time!

Using Internet search, Wikipedia, documentaries or library books to find answers to the following questions.

What were her goals?
_____
_____
_____
_____
_____

What did she actually accomplish?
_____
_____
_____
_____
_____
_____
_____

Who was her family, and was there anything notable about her upbringing?
_____
_____
_____

Was she married? If so, to whom, and is there anything significant about her spouse? _____
_____

What was her occupation?
_____
_____
_____

In what ways did her life affect our world?
_____
_____
_____
_____
_____
_____
_____

When and where was she born?
_____

When, where, and how did she die?
_____

How would the world be different if she had never been born?
_____
_____
_____
_____
_____
_____

What were her beliefs?
_____
_____
_____
_____
_____
_____
_____
_____
_____
_____

Design a postage stamp to commemorate this person

Random fact about this person:
_____
_____
_____
_____

A quote by this person:
_____
_____
_____
_____

Autobiography

Write a short auto biography from the perspective of the person you are studying.

_____
_____
_____
_____
_____
_____
_____
_____
_____
_____
_____
_____
_____
_____
_____
_____

You be the Judge

Illustrate their life

Now after all your research, would you say this person is a historic hero or villain? Explain in detail.

_____
_____
_____
_____
_____
_____
_____

Genghis Khan

Before you start, do you think this person is a hero of history or a villain?
_____

Why?
_____
_____
_____
_____

Draw this person

It's Research Time!

Using Internet search, Wikipedia, documentaries or library books to find answers to the following questions.

What were his goals?
_____
_____
_____
_____
_____

What did he actually accomplish?
_____
_____
_____
_____
_____
_____

Who was his family, and was there anything notable about his upbringing?
_____
_____
_____

Was he married? If so, to whom, and is there anything significant about his spouse? _____
_____

What was his occupation?
_____
_____
_____

In what ways did his life affect our world?
_____
_____
_____
_____
_____

When and where was he born?
_____

When, where, and how did he die?
_____
_____

How would the world be different if he had never been born?
_____
_____
_____
_____

What were his beliefs?
_____
_____
_____
_____
_____
_____
_____
_____

Design a postage stamp to commemorate this person

Random fact about this person:
_____
_____
_____

A quote by this person:
_____
_____
_____

Autobiography

Write a short auto biography from the perspective of the person you are studying.

_____
_____
_____
_____
_____
_____
_____
_____
_____
_____
_____
_____
_____
_____
_____
_____
_____
_____

You be the Judge

Illustrate their life

Now after all your research, would you say this person is a historic hero or villain? Explain in detail.

_____
_____
_____
_____
_____
_____

Dietrich Bonhoeffer

Before you start, do you think this person is a hero of history or a villain?

_____

Why?

_____
_____
_____
_____

Draw this person

It's Research Time!

Using Internet search, Wikipedia, documentaries or library books to find answers to the following questions.

What were his goals?
_____
_____
_____
_____
_____

What did he actually accomplish?
_____
_____
_____
_____
_____
_____
_____

Who was his family, and was there anything notable about his upbringing?
_____
_____
_____

Was he married? If so, to whom, and is there anything significant about his spouse? _____
_____

What was his occupation?
_____
_____
_____

In what ways did his life affect our world?
_____
_____
_____
_____
_____

When and where was he born?
___

When, where, and how did he die?
___
___

How would the world be different if he had never been born?
___
___
___
___

What were his beliefs?
___
___
___
___
___
___
___
___
___
___

Design a postage stamp to commemorate this person

Random fact about this person:
___
___
___

A quote by this person:
___
___
___

Autobiography

Write a short auto biography from the perspective of the person you are studying.

_____
_____
_____
_____
_____
_____
_____
_____
_____
_____
_____
_____
_____
_____
_____

You be the Judge

Illustrate their life

Now after all your research, would you say this person is a historic hero or villain? Explain in detail.

_____
_____
_____
_____
_____
_____
_____

Mozart

Before you start, do you think this person is a hero of history or a villain?
_____

Why?
_____
_____
_____
_____

Draw this person

It's Research Time!

Using Internet search, Wikipedia, documentaries or library books to find answers to the following questions.

What were his goals?
_____
_____
_____
_____
_____

What did he actually accomplish?
_____
_____
_____
_____
_____
_____

Who was his family, and was there anything notable about his upbringing?
_____
_____
_____

Was he married? If so, to whom, and is there anything significant about his spouse? _____
_____

What was his occupation?
_____
_____
_____

In what ways did his life affect our world?
_____
_____
_____
_____
_____

When and where was he born?
_____

When, where, and how did he die?
_____
_____

How would the world be different if he had never been born?
_____
_____
_____
_____
_____

What were his beliefs?
_____
_____
_____
_____
_____
_____
_____
_____
_____

Design a postage stamp to commemorate this person

Random fact about this person:
_____
_____
_____

A quote by this person:
_____
_____
_____

Autobiography

Write a short auto biography from the perspective of the person you are studying.

_____
_____
_____
_____
_____
_____
_____
_____
_____
_____
_____
_____
_____
_____

You be the Judge

Illustrate their life

Now after all your research, would you say this person is a historic hero or villain? Explain in detail.

_____
_____
_____
_____
_____
_____

Henry Ford

Before you start, do you think this person is a hero of history or a villain?

Why?

Draw this person

It's Research Time!

Using Internet search, Wikipedia, documentaries or library books to find answers to the following questions.

What were his goals?
_____
_____
_____
_____

What did he actually accomplish?
_____
_____
_____
_____
_____
_____

Who was his family, and was there anything notable about his upbringing?
_____
_____
_____

Was he married? If so, to whom, and is there anything significant about his spouse? _____
_____

What was his occupation?
_____
_____
_____

In what ways did his life affect our world?
_____
_____
_____
_____
_____

When and where was he born?

When, where, and how did he die?

How would the world be different if he had never been born?

What were his beliefs?

Random fact about this person:

A quote by this person:

Design a postage stamp to commemorate this person

Autobiography

Write a short auto biography from the perspective of the person you are studying.

_____
_____
_____
_____
_____
_____
_____
_____
_____
_____
_____
_____
_____
_____
_____
_____

You be the Judge

Illustrate their life

Now after all your research, would you say this person is a historic hero or villain? Explain in detail.

_____
_____
_____
_____
_____
_____

John Adams

Before you start, do you think this person is a hero of history or a villain?
_____

Why?
_____
_____
_____
_____

Draw this person

It's Research Time!

Using Internet search, Wikipedia, documentaries or library books to find answers to the following questions.

What were his goals?
_____
_____
_____
_____
_____

What did he actually accomplish?
_____
_____
_____
_____
_____
_____
_____

Who was his family, and was there anything notable about his upbringing?
_____
_____
_____

Was he married? If so, to whom, and is there anything significant about his spouse? _____
_____

What was his occupation?
_____
_____
_____

In what ways did his life affect our world?
_____
_____
_____
_____
_____

When and where was he born?
___

When, where, and how did he die?
___
___

How would the world be different if he had never been born?
___
___
___
___

What were his beliefs?
___
___
___
___
___
___
___
___

Design a postage stamp to commemorate this person

Random fact about this person:
___
___
___

A quote by this person:
___
___
___

Autobiography

Write a short auto biography from the perspective of the person you are studying.

_____
_____
_____
_____
_____
_____
_____
_____
_____
_____
_____
_____
_____
_____
_____
_____
_____

You be the Judge

Illustrate their life

Now after all your research, would you say this person is a historic hero or villain? Explain in detail.

_____
_____
_____
_____
_____
_____
_____

Saint Nicholas

Before you start, do you think this person is a hero of history or a villain?
_____

Why?
_____
_____
_____
_____

Draw this person

It's Research Time!

Using Internet search, Wikipedia, documentaries or library books to find answers to the following questions.

What were his goals?
_____
_____
_____
_____
_____

What did he actually accomplish?
_____
_____
_____
_____
_____
_____
_____

Who was his family, and was there anything notable about his upbringing?
_____
_____
_____

Was he married? If so, to whom, and is there anything significant about his spouse? _____
_____

What was his occupation?
_____
_____
_____

In what ways did his life affect our world?
_____
_____
_____
_____

When and where was he born?
_____

When, where, and how did he die?
_____
_____

How would the world be different if he had never been born?
_____
_____
_____
_____
_____

What were his beliefs?
_____
_____
_____
_____
_____
_____
_____
_____
_____

Design a postage stamp to commemorate this person

Random fact about this person:
_____
_____
_____

A quote by this person:
_____
_____
_____
_____

Autobiography

Write a short auto biography from the perspective of the person you are studying.

_____
_____
_____
_____
_____
_____
_____
_____
_____
_____
_____
_____
_____
_____
_____
_____
_____

You be the Judge

Illustrate their life

Now after all your research, would you say this person is a historic hero or villain? Explain in detail.

_____
_____
_____
_____
_____
_____
_____

Pol Pot

Before you start, do you think this person is a hero of history or a villain?
_____

Why?
_____
_____
_____
_____

Draw this person

It's Research Time!

Using Internet search, Wikipedia, documentaries or library books to find answers to the following questions.

What were his goals?
_____
_____
_____
_____
_____

What did he actually accomplish?
_____
_____
_____
_____
_____
_____

Who was his family, and was there anything notable about his upbringing?
_____
_____
_____

Was he married? If so, to whom, and is there anything significant about his spouse? _____
_____

What was his occupation?
_____
_____
_____

In what ways did his life affect our world?
_____
_____
_____
_____
_____

When and where was he born?
_____

When, where, and how did he die?
_____
_____

How would the world be different if he had never been born?
_____
_____
_____
_____

What were his beliefs?
_____
_____
_____
_____
_____
_____
_____
_____

Design a postage stamp to commemorate this person

Random fact about this person:
_____
_____
_____

A quote by this person:
_____
_____
_____
_____

Autobiography

Write a short auto biography from the perspective of the person you are studying.

_____
_____
_____
_____
_____
_____
_____
_____
_____
_____
_____
_____
_____
_____
_____
_____
_____
_____
_____

You be the Judge

Illustrate their life

Now after all your research, would you say this person is a historic hero or villain? Explain in detail.

_____
_____
_____
_____
_____
_____
_____

David Livingstone

Before you start, do you think this person is a hero of history or a villain?
_____

Why?
_____
_____
_____
_____

Draw this person

It's Research Time!

Using Internet search, Wikipedia, documentaries or library books to find answers to the following questions.

What were his goals?
_____
_____
_____
_____
_____

What did he actually accomplish?
_____
_____
_____
_____
_____
_____
_____

Who was his family, and was there anything notable about his upbringing?
_____
_____
_____

Was he married? If so, to whom, and is there anything significant about his spouse? _____
_____

What was his occupation?
_____
_____
_____

In what ways did his life affect our world?
_____
_____
_____
_____
_____

When and where was he born?
_____

When, where, and how did he die?
_____
_____

How would the world be different if he had never been born?
_____
_____
_____
_____

What were his beliefs?
_____
_____
_____
_____
_____
_____
_____
_____

Design a postage stamp to commemorate this person

Random fact about this person:
_____
_____
_____

A quote by this person:
_____
_____
_____

Autobiography

Write a short auto biography from the perspective of the person you are studying.

_____
_____
_____
_____
_____
_____
_____
_____
_____
_____
_____
_____
_____
_____
_____
_____
_____

You be the Judge

Illustrate their life

Now after all your research, would you say this person is a historic hero or villain? Explain in detail.

_____
_____
_____
_____
_____
_____
_____

Neil Armstrong

Before you start, do you think this person is a hero of history or a villain?

Why?

Draw this person

It's Research Time!

Using Internet search, Wikipedia, documentaries or library books to find answers to the following questions.

What were his goals?
_____
_____
_____
_____
_____

What did he actually accomplish?
_____
_____
_____
_____
_____
_____

Who was his family, and was there anything notable about his upbringing?
_____
_____
_____

Was he married? If so, to whom, and is there anything significant about his spouse? _____
_____

What was his occupation?
_____
_____
_____

In what ways did his life affect our world?
_____
_____
_____
_____
_____

When and where was he born?
_____

When, where, and how did he die?
_____
_____

How would the world be different if he had never been born?
_____
_____
_____
_____

What were his beliefs?
_____
_____
_____
_____
_____
_____
_____
_____

Design a postage stamp to commemorate this person

Random fact about this person:
_____
_____
_____

A quote by this person:
_____
_____
_____
_____

Autobiography

Write a short auto biography from the perspective of the person you are studying.

_____
_____
_____
_____
_____
_____
_____
_____
_____
_____
_____
_____
_____
_____
_____
_____
_____

You be the Judge

Illustrate their life

Now after all your research, would you say this person is a historic hero or villain? Explain in detail.

_____
_____
_____
_____
_____
_____

John Jay

Before you start, do you think this person is a hero of history or a villain?

_____

Why?

_____
_____
_____
_____

Draw this person

It's Research Time!

Using Internet search, Wikipedia, documentaries or library books to find answers to the following questions.

What were his goals?
_____
_____
_____
_____
_____

What did he actually accomplish?
_____
_____
_____
_____
_____
_____
_____

Who was his family, and was there anything notable about his upbringing?
_____
_____
_____

Was he married? If so, to whom, and is there anything significant about his spouse? _____
_____

What was his occupation?
_____
_____
_____

In what ways did his life affect our world?
_____
_____
_____
_____
_____

When and where was he born?
_____

When, where, and how did he die?
_____
_____

How would the world be different if he had never been born?
_____
_____
_____
_____

What were his beliefs?
_____
_____
_____
_____
_____
_____
_____
_____
_____
_____

Design a postage stamp to commemorate this person

Random fact about this person:
_____
_____
_____

A quote by this person:
_____
_____
_____
_____

Autobiography

Write a short auto biography from the perspective of the person you are studying.

_____
_____
_____
_____
_____
_____
_____
_____
_____
_____
_____
_____
_____
_____
_____
_____
_____
_____
_____

You be the Judge

Illustrate their life

Now after all your research, would you say this person is a historic hero or villain? Explain in detail.

_____
_____
_____
_____
_____
_____
_____
_____

Resources Used in Research:

Additional Notes:

What Is Fun-Schooling?

Fun-schooling is a one-of-a-kind way to learn. It is tapping into kids interests while covering all the major subjects. Fun-schooling is for creative learners, students with learning disabilities, gifted students, and everyone in between. It's a way for students to learn without the stress, pressure, and boredom of other methods. We started out creating materials for our children. Then friends and family wanted to try it out. Before we knew it, Fun-schooling with Thinking Tree Books was born!

Fun-Schooling With Thinking Tree Books

Copyright Information

Thinking Tree Fun-Schooling Books, and electronic printable downloads are for home and family use only. You may make copies of these materials for only the children in your household.

All other uses of this material must be permitted in writing by Thinking Tree LLC. It is a violation of copyright law to distribute the electronic files or make copies for your friends, associates or students without. For information on using these materials for businesses, co-ops, summer camps, day camps, daycare, afterschool program, churches, or schools please contact us for licensing.

Contact Us:
The Thinking Tree LLC
+1 (USA)   317.622.8852
info@funschooling.com

Made in the USA
Las Vegas, NV
17 August 2023

76235481R00116